AF588017

PEGASUS ENCYCLOPEDIA LIBRARY

Physics

WORK, FORCE AND ENERGY

Edited by: Anil Kumar Tomar, Pallabi B. Tomar
Managing editor: Tapasi De
Designed by: Vijesh Chahal, Anil Kumar and Rohit Kumar
Illustrated by: Suman S. Roy, Tanoy Choudhury
Colouring done by: Vinay Kumar, Sonu, Kiran Kumari & Pradeep Kumar

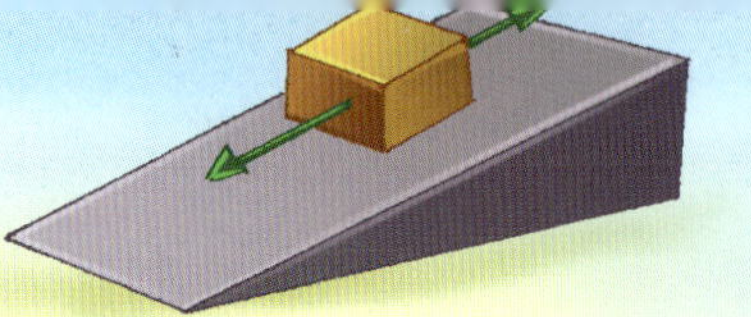
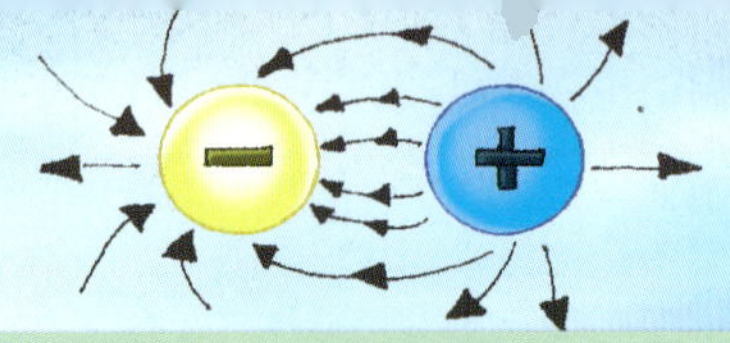

CONTENTS

What is force?

All of us know that some effort is required to put a stationary object into motion or to stop a moving object. In our everyday life, we experience this as a muscular effort and say that we must push or pull an object to change its state of motion. The concept of any type of force is based on this push or pull. Thus, in the simplest form, we can define a force as,

"Anything that can cause a change to any state of objects is called force."

Forces can change the shape of an object, change the speed, move or stop an object or change the direction of a moving object. Forces can simply be classified as contact forces and non-contact forces. A contact force must be in contact with an object to cause a change, such as to push or pull things. A non-contact force does not have to touch an object to cause a change, such as electric and magnetic forces, gravitational forces etc.

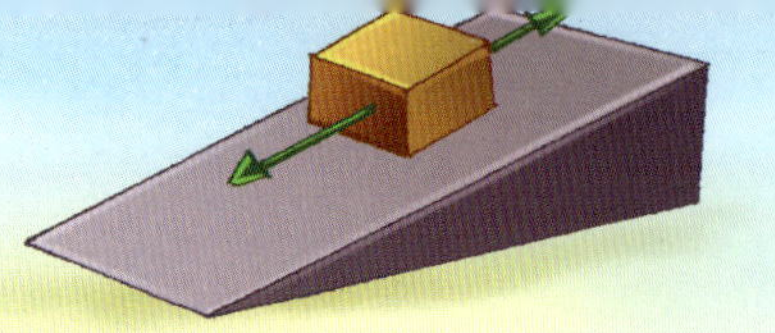

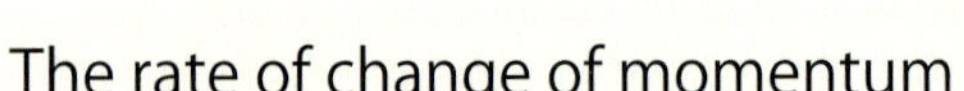

Second law of motion and force

Newton's second law of motion states that,

"The rate of change of linear momentum of a body is directly proportional to the external unbalanced force acting on it".

Now, suppose an object of mass m, is moving in a straight line with an initial velocity u. A constant force F is applied on it which accelerates it uniformly to velocity v in time t.

Then, the initial and final momentum of the object will be,

$$p_1 = mu$$

$$p_2 = mv$$

The change in momentum

$$= p_2 - p_1$$

$$= mv - mu$$

$$= m \times (v - u)$$

The rate of change of momentum

$$= m \times (v - u)/t$$

Now, according to second law of motion,

Force $\propto$ rate of change of momentum

$$F \propto m \times (v - u)/t$$

$$F = k\,m \times (v - u)/t$$

The quantity, k is a constant of proportionality.

We know that, acceleration is the rate of change of velocity.

$$a = (v - u)/t$$

On putting a in the above equation, we get

$$F = k\,m\,a$$

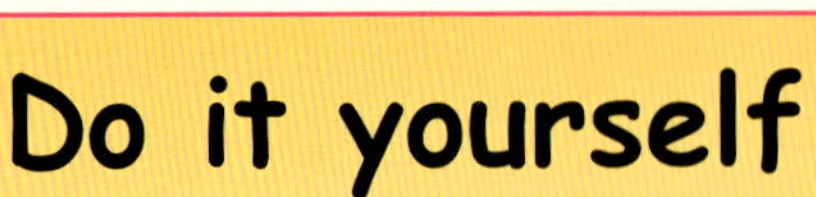

Do it yourself

What falls faster?: Stand on a sturdy table or on a high chair and drop two objects at the same time—a heavy object and a light one.

Result: Both reach the ground at the same time.

Explanation: The weight of an object does not affect its speed as it falls. But we know that a feather doesn't fall as fast as a stone and that a man with a parachute falls more slowly than a man without one. The shape of the feather and the parachute are important because they are slowed down by the air's resistance.

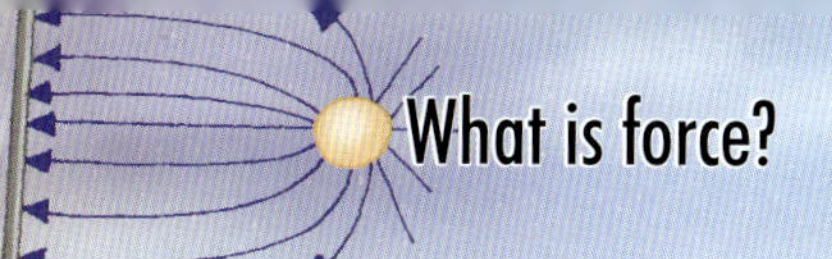

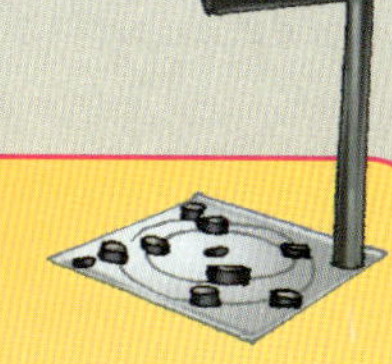

Do it yourself

Falling objects do work: Lift a little pebble and a large stone from the floor and place each on a table. Lay a flat tin can on the floor near the table. Push off the pebble so that it strikes the can. What happens? Push off the large stone so that it strikes the can. What happens?

Result: The large stone makes a large dent in the can while the pebble barely scratches it.

Explanation: The large stone stores up more energy. It took more energy to lift it than it did to lift the little stone. Objects which require more energy to lift have more energy when they fall.

The SI units of mass and acceleration are kg and m s^{-2} respectively. The unit of force is so chosen that the value of the constant, k becomes one. For this, one unit of force is defined as the amount that produces an acceleration of 1 m s^{-2} in an object of 1 kg mass. That is,

1 unit of force = $k \times (1 \text{ kg}) \times (1 \text{ m s}^{-2})$. Thus, the value of k becomes 1. So force can be calculated as,

$$F = ma$$

The Newton's first law of motion can easily be understood mathematically from this expression of force.

$$F = ma$$

$$= m \times (v - u)/t$$

If we rearrange this equation, we will get

$$Ft = mv - mu$$

Thus, when $F = 0$, $v = u$ for whatever time, t is taken. This indicates that an object will continue moving with uniform velocity u throughout the time. If an object is at rest that is, its initial velocity (u) is zero then the final velocity (v) will also be zero. That is, the object will remain at rest.

The unit of force is kg m s^{-2} or Newton, which has the symbol N. This unit is named after Sir Isaac Newton who first defined force. Force is a vector quantity and has a magnitude and a direction.

Due to gravitational effects, you weigh slightly less when the moon is directly overhead.

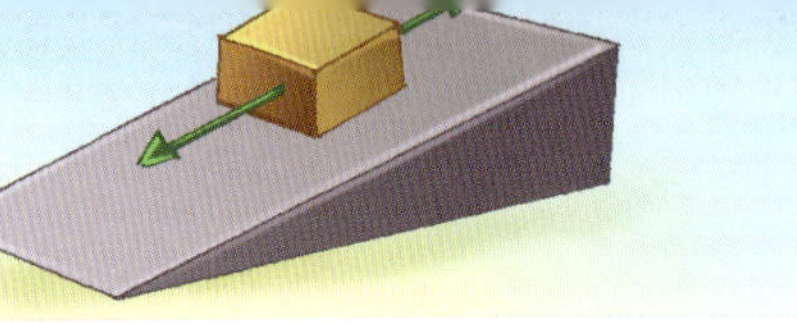

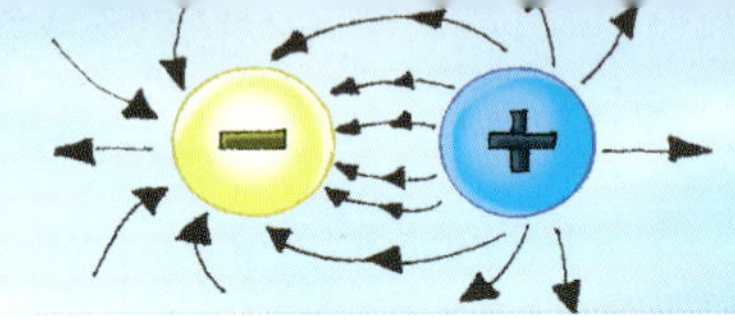

Example: A force of 50 N gives a mass m1, an acceleration of 10 m s^{-2} and a mass m_2, an acceleration of 20 m s^{-2}. If we tie both of the masses together, what acceleration would the same force give?

Solution:

For first mass (m_1),

Force, $F = 50$ N

Acceleration, $a = 10 \text{ m s}^{-2}$

We know that,

$$F = ma$$

$$m = F/a$$

$$= 50/10$$

$$= 5 \text{ kg}$$

Thus, mass of first object is 5kg.

For second mass (m_2),

Force, $F = 50$ N

Acceleration, $a = 20 \text{ m s}^{-2}$

We know that,

$$F = ma$$

$$m = F/a$$

$$= 50/20$$

$$= 2.5 \text{ kg}$$

Thus, mass of second object is 2.5kg.

Total mass of two objects = 5 + 2.5 = 7.5 kg

From above equation we have, $a = F/m$

$$= 50/7.5 \text{ m s}^{-2}$$

$$= 6.66 \text{ m s}^{-2}$$

Thus, the force will give 6.66 m s^{-2} acceleration if both masses are tied together.

Forces in Physics

In real life, we experience different types of forces every day. Physics defines many different types of forces but all are described and calculated in the same way. The major forces are:

Gravitational forces

Gravitational forces are the most important forces in the universe. These are defined as the attractive forces between two objects due to their mass. Newton, upon observing an apple fall from a tree, thought that the apple is accelerated, since its velocity changes from zero as it is hanging on the tree and moves toward the ground. Thus, according to his second law of motion, there must be a force that acts on the apple to cause this acceleration. Newton concluded that any two objects in the Universe exert gravitational attraction on each other. According to him, the force holding any object to the Earth is the same as the force holding the moon, the planets and other heavenly bodies in their orbits. He proposed the universal law of gravitation, stating **"Every object in the universe attracts every other object with a force which is proportional to the product of their masses and inversely proportional to the square of the distance between them."**

Electromagnetic forces

Almost all of the forces that we experience n everyday life are electromagnetic forces. Electromagnetic forces are the forces between

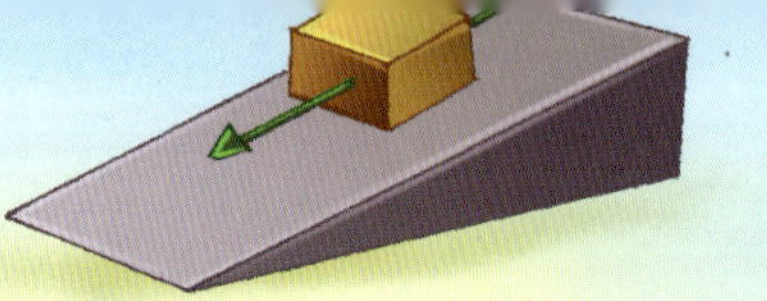

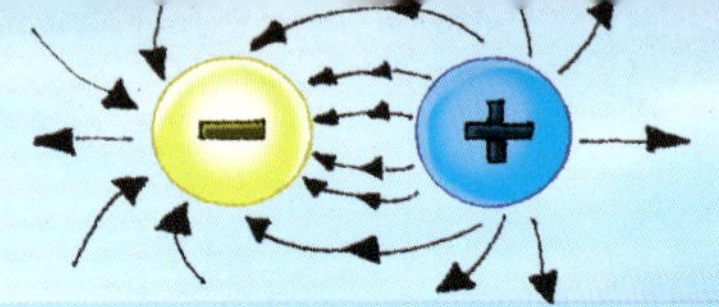

electrical charges and currents. Our most direct access to these forces is through electric circuits. The lightning during thunderstorms is also an example of electromagnetic forces. The electromagnetic forces are exerted when electric current flows through a conductor.

Electrostatic forces

Electrostatic force is experienced by two charges when they are placed together in a system. The force exerted by non-moving that is, static charges on each other is called the electrostatic force. The like charges always repel each other while opposite charges attract each other. Thus, the electrostatic force between the like charges is repulsive in nature while it is attractive between opposite charges. Coulomb's law is the quantitative measure of these forces between two point charges. This law states that **"The force between two point charges is inversely proportional to the square of the distance between the charges and directly proportional to the product of the magnitude of the two charges. This force acts along the line joining the two charges".**

Magnetic forces

Magnetism is defined as the force exerted by a magnetic object, through its magnetic field, on another object in its magnetic field. The two objects do not essentially need to be physically attached for the force to be exerted. Objects feel the magnetic force due to the surrounding magnetic field. The magnets have a pair of opposite poles, called north (N) and south (S). If we cut the magnet into tiny pieces, each piece will have both the poles N and S. These poles always occur in pairs. In nature, we can never find a north magnetic pole or south

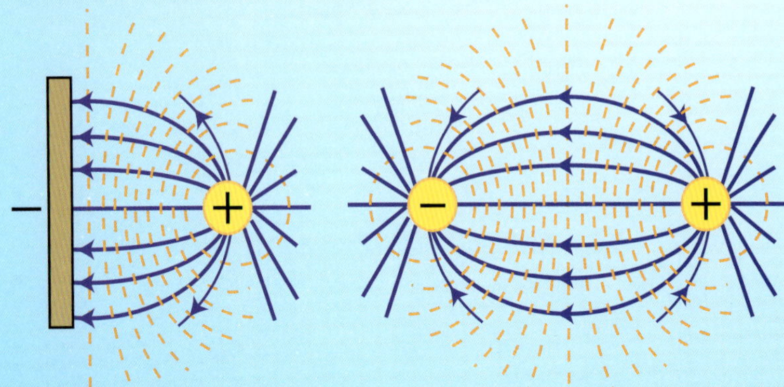

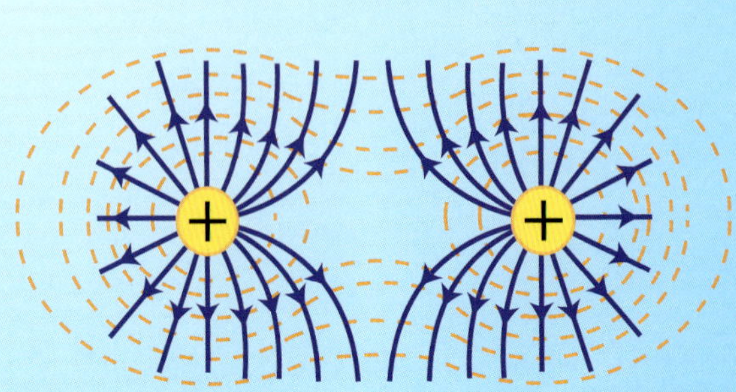

magnetic pole on its own.

Like poles of magnets always repel each other while unlike poles attract. So, two N poles or two S poles push away from each other while N pole and S pole attract each other.

Friction

The friction between two surfaces retards the motion of an object and finally brings it to rest. Friction arises due to the interaction of the two surfaces. Irregularities in the structure of the matters causes friction force. These irregularities can be detected in micro dimensions. Friction force is always opposite to the direction of motion and tends to decrease net force. Friction is electromagnetic in origin. In the moving parts of machines a minimum of friction is desired. An excess of friction produces heat, which in turn causes expansion, the locking of the moving parts, and a consequent breakdown of the machinery. Lubrication and ball bearings minimize friction.

Drag forces

This is the force experienced by an object when travelling through a medium like an aeroplane flying in air. When something travels through the air it needs to displace air as it travels. In response to this, the air also exerts a force on the object. The drag force is very useful for flyers that make parachute

Friction

Gravity

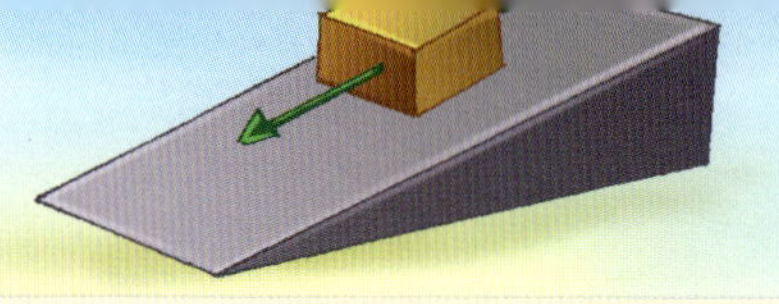

jumps. They jump from high altitudes and if there would be no drag force, they would continue accelerating all the way to the ground. The drag force is proportional to the area of the object. Thus, parachutes are made wide so that the more surface results in greater drag force. Due to this, it slowly comes to the ground.

Internal and external forces

Forces can be categorized as internal forces or external forces.

The importance of categorizing a force as being either internal or external is related to the ability of that type of force to change an object's total mechanical energy when it does work upon an object.

External forces when work upon an object, they change the total mechanical energy (KE + PE) of that object. If the work is positive work, then the object will gain energy. If the work is negative work, then the object will lose energy. The gain or loss in energy can be in the form of potential energy, kinetic energy, or both. The work done will be equal to the change in mechanical energy of the object. Because external forces are capable of changing the total mechanical energy of an object, they are referred as non-conservative forces. The external forces include the applied force, normal force, tension force, friction force, and air resistance.

When an internal force acts on an object, the total mechanical energy of that object remains constant. In such cases, the energy of the object is converted into different form. For example, when an object falls from high elevation to a lower elevation by gravity, some of the potential energy of that object is transformed into kinetic energy. But, the sum of the kinetic and potential energies remains constant. Thus, these forces are sometimes referred as conservative forces. The internal forces include the gravity forces, magnetic force, electrical forceand spring force.

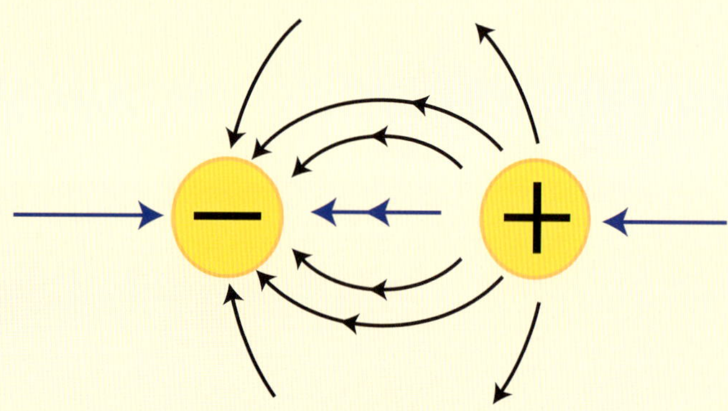

Frictional force

Newton's first law of motion states that,

"An object continues to be in its state of rest or uniform motion along a straight line until or unless an external force acts on it."

If we apply this on a rolling ball moving on a horizontal surface, it should continue to move indefinitely as no force is acting on it. But this does not happen practically. The speed of the ball decreases continuously and eventually it comes to the rest after a certain period of time. The ball stops because of the force exerted by the surface on the ball. This force opposes the motion of the ball or we can say that the ball experiences a force, which opposes its motion. This force is known as the force of friction. Thus, the force of friction or simply friction is defined as the force which opposes the motion of an object over another object in contact with it.

The friction between two surfaces retards the motion of an object and finally brings it to rest. Thus, an external force must be applied continuously on the moving object in order to maintain the uniform motion of the object. This force must be equal and opposite to the force of friction.

The surfaces of bodies are never perfectly smooth. Even the smooth surfaces have depressions and projections. The interlocking of the irregularities of the surfaces in contact causes friction. The friction is considered as a self-adjusting force. Let us consider a case of an object lying on a surface and we apply a force on it to displace it. The friction has an amazing property of adjusting its magnitude so as to become equal to the applied force tending to produce motion. However, after a certain limit, the force of friction cannot increase further. If the applied force exceeds this particular limit then the object starts moving. The maximum value of the force of friction, which acts on an object when it just begins to move over the surface of another object is known as the limiting friction.

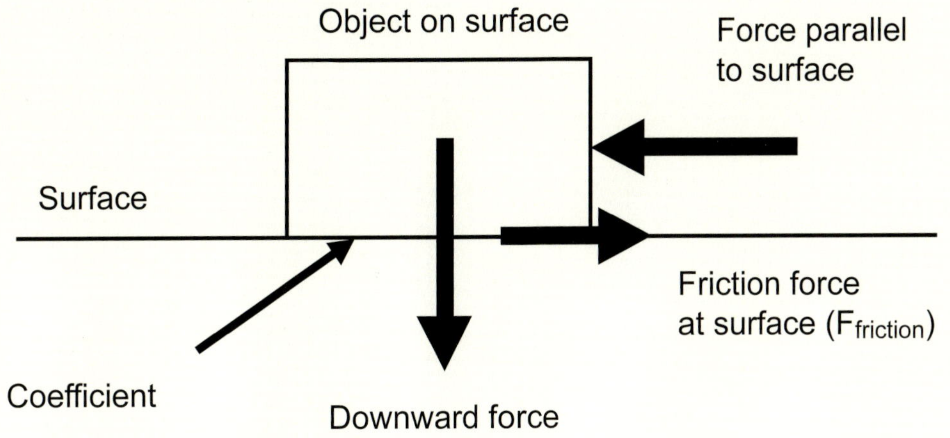

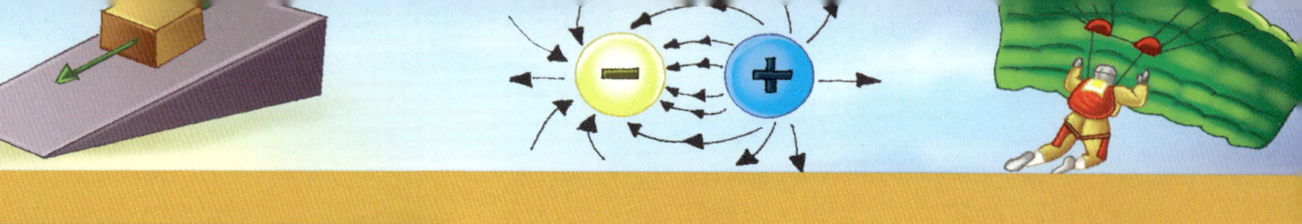

Types of friction

Static friction comes into play when there is no relative motion between the two surfaces in contact.

Sliding friction is the force required to keep the body in steady motion after the motion has once started on the surface of another object. The sliding friction is smaller than the limiting friction.

Rolling Friction is developed between the surfaces when a body rolls over a surface.

Methods for decreasing friction

Friction can be decreased by the following methods:

1. Lubricants like oil or grease can reduce friction.
2. Ball bearings and roller bearings are used for decreasing rolling friction.
3. Anti-friction metals or alloys are used for reducing sliding friction.

4. By polishing the surfaces, the friction between the moving surfaces can be reduced.

Applications of friction

1. We are able to walk on the surface of the Earth due to friction.
2. The fibres of threads are held together due to friction.
3. The brakes applied in automobiles work by friction.
4. Nails and screws are based on the principle of friction.

Disadvantage of force of friction

The biggest disadvantage of friction is that a lot of energy is wasted in the form of heat. Friction causes wear and tear of the moving parts of an object.

Do it yourself

Why do we use wheels?: Borrow an oil drum or small barrel for this experiment. Place the barrel in an up- right position and push it across the room. Then turn it on its side and roll it back.

Result: It is much easier to roll, than to push the can.

Explanation: There is less rolling friction than sliding friction. In sliding, the bumps on the rough surfaces catch against each other. In rolling, the bumps of the wheel roll over the bumps of the rough surface without rubbing as much.

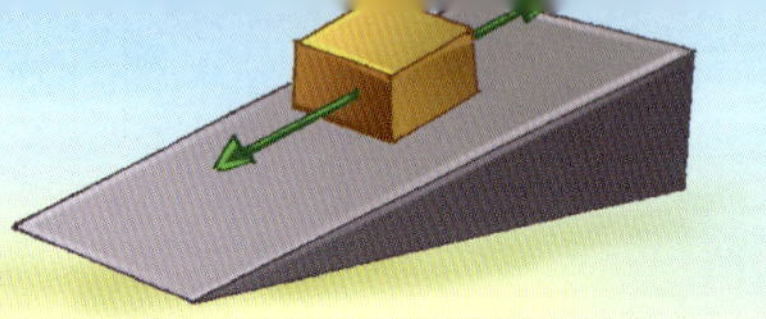
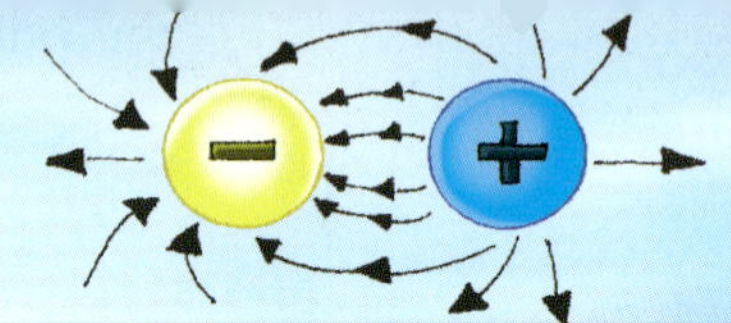

Gravitational force

Gravitational force is the attractive force which exists between any two objects that have mass. The force of gravitation pulls objects together. The gravitational force is observed in all objects in the universe, from the largest galaxies down to the smallest atoms. Thus, it is also regarded as universal gravitation. Newton was the first scientist who proposed this force. According to him, the force holding any object to the Earth is the same as the force holding the moon, the planets and other heavenly bodies in their orbits. He proposed the universal law of gravitation whichlaw states that,

"Every object in the universe attracts every other object with a force (gravitational pull) which is proportional to the product of their masses and inversely proportional to the square of the distance between them."

This gravitational force acts along the line joining the centres of two objects. Mathematically, this force is given by:

$$F = G * mM/R^2$$

Where, F is the force between two masses (in Newtons)

m and M are the two masses (in kilograms)

R is the distance between the centres of these masses (in metres)

G is the universal constant of gravitation (6.7 x 10-11 Nm2/kg2)

Why do things fall down?

Suspend various things from strings-a marble, a can, a ball and a toy. Cut each string. You will see that the objects fall as soon as you cut their string.

Explanation: The force of gravity pulls objects towards the centre of the earth. This pull of gravity sometimes helps us and sometimes works against us. Gravity keeps us and everything around us from flying off into space. It also makes it harder for us to send a rocket to the space. Gravity keeps Earth and the other planets in our solar system in orbit around the Sun. It also keeps the Moon in orbit around Earth. Tides are caused by the rotation of the Earth and the gravitational effects of the Moon and Sun.

Important facts about gravitational force

Gravitation is actually a very weak force. The pull is too weak to be felt between two masses of comparable size. It is only when one of the masses is the size of a planet that we can feel the force of gravity.

The huge gravitational force of our nearest star, the Sun, holds together the nine planets of our Solar System.

Gravity is defined as the gravitational force that occurs between the Earth and other bodies. Gravity is the force which pulls objects towards the Earth. That's why fruits fall on ground from the tree.

Gravity holds us on the ground and causes objects to fall back to the ground after being thrown in the air.

The Earth's gravitational pull extends out into space in all directions. As we move away from the centre of the Earth, the gravitational pull becomes weaker.

The weight of an object is the force of gravity on that object. The weight of an object changes depending on its location in the universe.

Mass and weight of an object

The mass of an object is measured in terms of inertia. Inertia is the natural tendency of an object to resist a change in its state of motion or of rest. The mass of an object is directly proportional to its inertia. It remains the same everywhere, whether the object is on the Earth, the Moon or in outer space. Therefore, the mass of an object is always constant and does not change from place to place.

The weight of an object is defined as the force with which it is attracted towards the Earth. We know that the Earth attracts every object with a certain force and this force depends on the mass (*m*) of the object and the acceleration due to the gravity (g).

We know that force is expressed as,

$F = m \times a$

If we replace acceleration by acceleration due to gravity, we get

$F = m \times g$

This force of attraction is the weight of the object. It is denoted by 'W' and can be expressed as,

$F = m \times g$

The unit of weight is the same as that of force, Newton (N). The weight is a force acting vertically downwards; it has both magnitude and direction. We know that the value of g is constant at a given place. Therefore at a given place, the weight of an object is directly proportional to the mass. Also, we know that the value of 'g' varies at different places; the weight of an object also varies accordingly. That's why the weight of a body at Moon is very less than at the Earth.

If you yelled for 8 years, 7 months and 6 days, you would have produced just enough sound energy to heat up one cup of coffee.

Work

When a force acts upon an object to cause a displacement of the object, it is said that work was done upon the object. There are three key ingredients to work—force, displacement, and cause. In order for a force to qualify as having done work on an object, there must be a displacement cased by the force. In each case there is a force exerted upon an object to cause the displacement.

We shall first consider the case when the force is acting in the direction of displacement. Let a constant force, *F* act on an object.

Let the object be displaced through a distance, *d* in the direction of the force. Let *W* be the work done. In the simplest form, we define work as the product of the force and displacement. Mathematically,

$$\text{Work done} = \text{force} \times \text{displacement}$$

$$W = F\, d$$

Thus, work done by force acting on an object is equal to the magnitude of the force multiplied by the distance moved in the direction of the force. The unit of work is Newton metre (N m) or joule (J). If F = 1 N and d = 1 m, then the work done by the force will be 1 N m. Thus, 1 J is the amount of work done on an object when a force of 1 N displaces it by 1 m along the line of action of the force.

If the direction of the force acting is different than that of the displacement caused by it, then work can be expressed by the following equation:

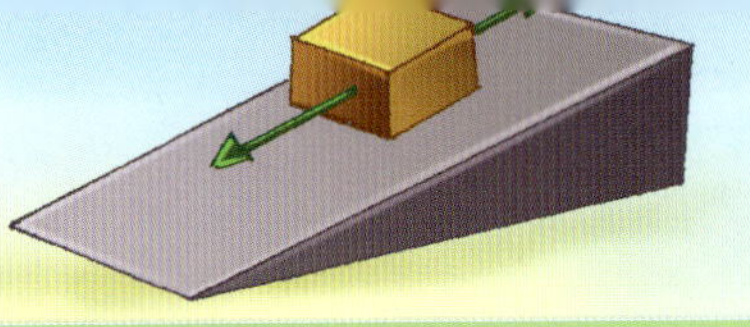
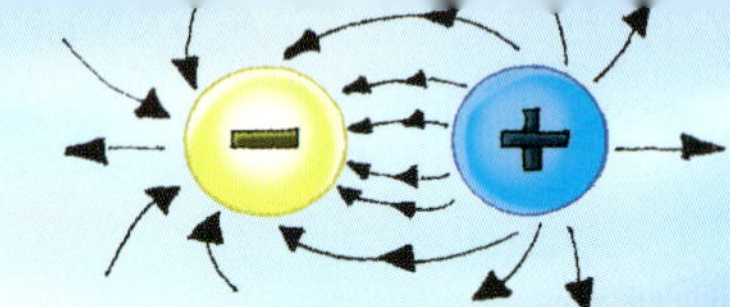

$W = F.d.\cos\Theta$

Where, the angle Θ (theta) is defined as the angle between the force and the displacement vector.

Example: A man lifts a bag of 20 kg from the ground and puts it on a height 2 m above the ground. Calculate the work done by him on the bag. Use $g = 10\ m/s^2$

Solution:

Mass of bag,

$m = 20$ kg and

Displacement,

$d = 2$ m

Work done by man can be calculated using equation,

$W = F * d$

We know that force,

$F = m\,a$

Here, acceleration is g (that is, acceleration due to gravity)

Thus,

$F = mg$ and above equation becomes

$W = mg * d$

$= 20\ kg \times 10\ m/s^2 \times 2\ m$

$= 400\ J$

Thus, work done by man to lift bag is 400 J.

Do it yourself

Why do we oil machines?: Slide two blocks of wood over each other. Then rub soap or petroleum jelly over each surface, and slide the blocks over each other again.

Result: The surfaces slide more easily after the soap is put on.

Explanation: The lubricants reduce friction between the surfaces of objects.

What is energy?

Life cannot be imagined without energy. If somebody asks where energy comes from, the first reply is the Sun. Sun is the biggest natural source of energy as many of our energy sources are derived from the sun. Energy can be defined as the ability to do work. This is the energy which transformed into work when we burn fuel to move something like a car. The energy of fuel is generally stored energy which is used to do work. The energy possessed by an object is thus measured in terms of its capacity of doing work. The unit of energy is, therefore, the same as that of work, that is, joule (J). 1 Joule is the energy required to do 1 joule of work.

People have learned to use stored energy to do useful work for them. By burning coal, we can use the chemical energy stored in the coal to heat up water until it becomes steam which then drives large machines to generate electricity. Electricity is another form of energy and it can be made to do useful work, like running your washing machine or powering your computer and other electronic devices. It can be made from renewable energy sources like wind and water. It can also be made by nuclear power, yet another source of energy.

An object that possesses energy can exert a force on another object. When this happens, energy is transferred from the former to the latter. The second object may move as it receives energy and therefore do some work. This implies that any object that possesses energy can do work. The object which does the work loses energy and the object on which the work is done gains energy.

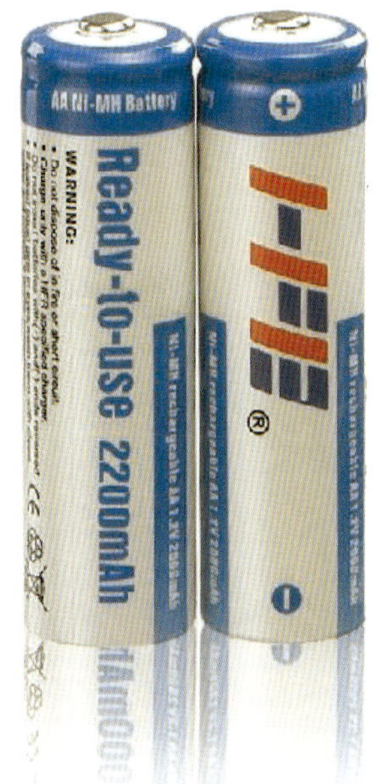

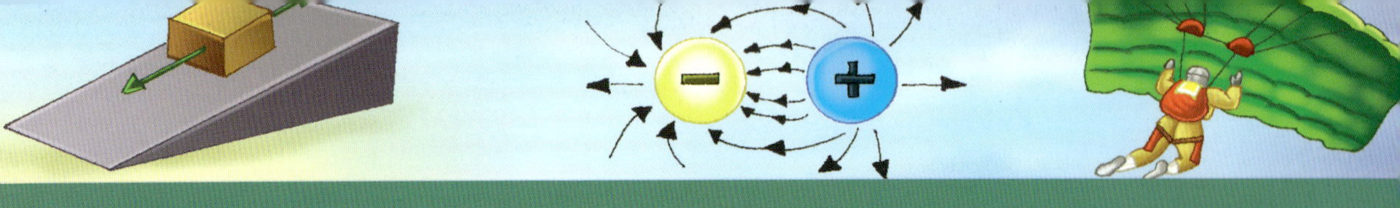

Potential energy

Potential energy is the stored energy of an object at rest. The energy which is transferred to an object is stored as potential energy if it is not used to cause a change in the velocity or speed of the object. It is called so because, in its current form, it is not doing any work or causing any change in its surroundings. However, it has the potential to do work or to be converted into different forms of energy, such as kinetic energy. The standard unit for measuring such energy is the joule.

When we displace an object from its original position and there is energy pulling it back to that position, potential energy tends to exist. For example, a ball at the end of a spring has potential energy that will be converted to kinetic energy when allowed to return to its original position. A weight held above the ground always has potential energy as gravity which pulls it back to its original position when released.

The most important principle of potential energy is the law of conservation of energy. This law states that energy can neither be created nor destroyed. The energy always transfers from one form to another. The energy used to do some work never

Do it yourself

Energy changes from one form to another: Feel a nail and hammer. Then hammer the nail into a piece of wood. Feel both nail and hammer again.

Result: Both nail and hammer are warm.

Explanation: The muscle energy transfers to the moving hammer, and goes from the hammer to the nail. This energy converts to the heat which makes nail and hammer warm.

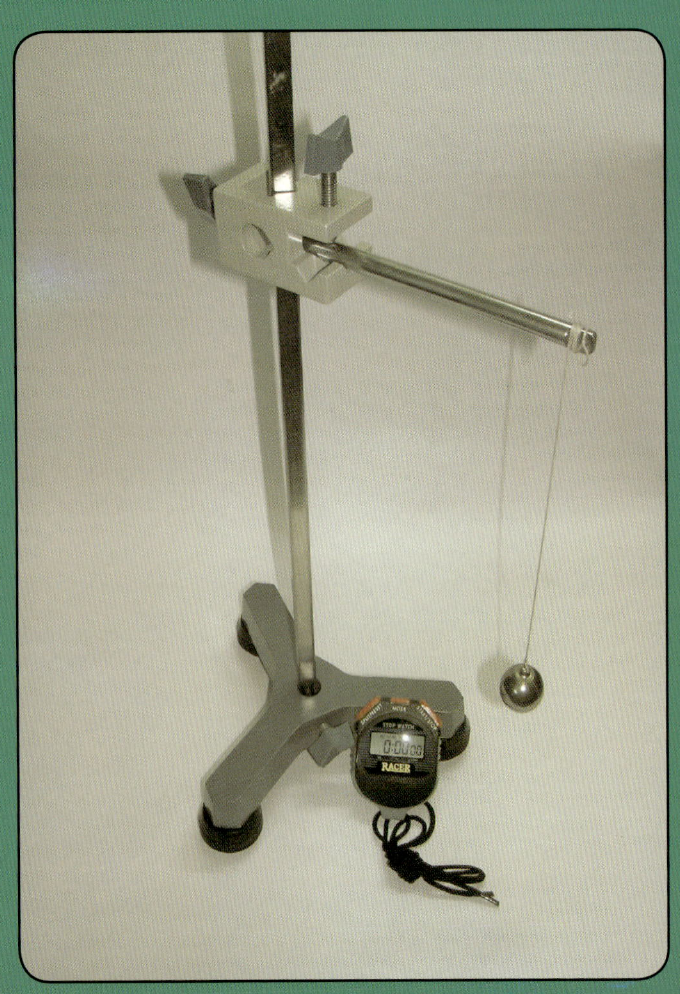

disappears but it changes to another form. For example, the work done to lift something is 'stored"' as potential energy. It is then released as kinetic energy by a restoring force. The energy input is always equal to the energy output; there is no gain or loss in overall energy.

Different forms of potential energy

There are many different types of potential energy. Some of the important forms of potential energy are:

Potential chemical energy is related to the chemical bonds in a molecule. In chemical reactions, it is transformed to other forms of energy as the bonds are broken and reformed. This energy is stored in things like the food, chemicals, drugs, fuels and explosives.

Potential elastic energy exists in elastic objects, such as a bow or rubber band. This energy is stored in stressed condition which is converted to kinetic energy when stretched.

Gravitational potential energy of a body is due to the gravitational pull of another large body, like a planet. The potential energy of objects on Earth is due to gravitational pull of the Earth.

Potential electrical energy can be described in three different forms forms— electrostatic, electrodynamic and nuclear. Potential electrostatic energy exists in charged particle at rest. These particles experience this potential energy because of their position in relation to other charged particles. Potential electrodynamic energy exists because of electromagnetic field moving charged particles. This electromagnetic field has the potential to move other objects. Potential nuclear energy exists due to interaction of subatomic particles, such as protons, electrons, and neutrons, in the nucleus of atoms. Nuclear energy is stored in the nucleus of atoms. This energy is used in nuclear power stations to generate heat. The Sun and all the other stars shine because of the energy released when atomic nuclei split or fuse together.

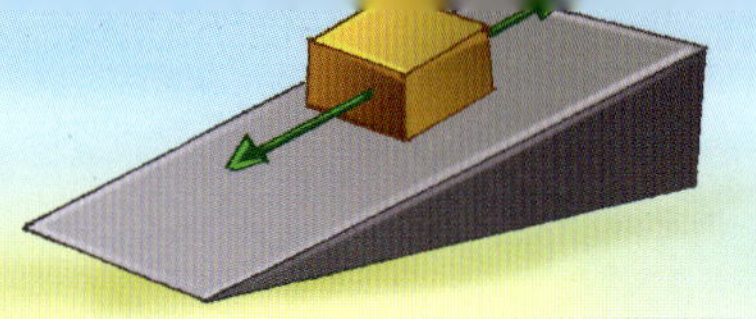
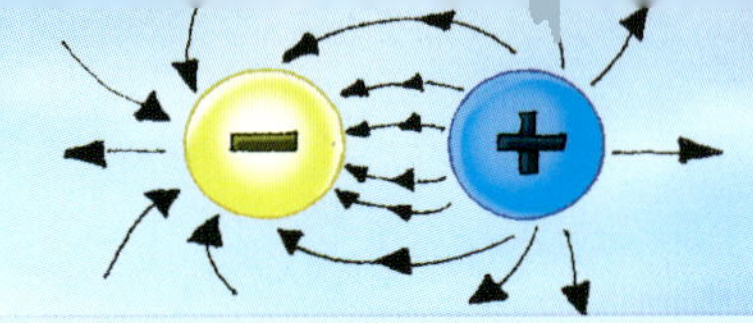

Potential energy of an object at height

Energy of an object increases when it is raised through a height. The energy increases because work is done on it against gravity while it is being raised. The amount of increased energy is equal to the work done to raise its height. The energy present in such an object is known as the gravitational potential energy. Thus, the **gravitational potential energy** of an object at a point above the ground can be defined as the work done in raising it from the ground to that height against gravity of Earth. This can be used to derive an expression for the gravitational potential energy of an object at a height.

Let us consider that an object of mass '*m*' is raised to a height '*h*' from the ground. The minimum force required to raise the object is equal to the weight of the object (*mg*). We know that, the object gains energy equal to the work done on it.

The work done on the object against gravity can be expressed as,

Work done, W = force × displacement

$= mg \times h$

$= mgh$

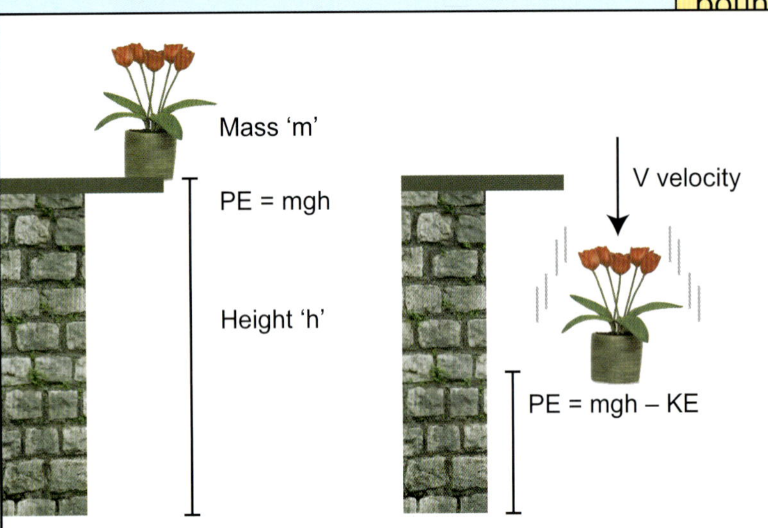

Elastic and inelastic collisions

In elastic collisions the kinetic energy (KE) is conserved. In inelastic collisions, the KE goes somewhere. Where? Collect about 50 bouncy balls and a bucket. Place the empty bucket on the floor in front of you. Drop a ball into it from about chest height. Now put some of the balls into the bucket and again drop the ball. Finally, put all the balls into the bucket and again drop the ball.

Result: When you drop the ball in empty bucket, it bounces back up to you, out of the bucket. It bounces back much lower when there are few balls inside and possibly it may knock another ball out. But it stops more or less dead and does not bounce out when all balls are inside.

Explanation: In empty bucket, the ball has little to share its kinetic energy (KE) with. When it is partly filled with balls, the ball loses some of its KE by colliding with one or two other balls of similar mass but when there are many balls which rapidly share the KE, the original ball makes many quick collisions and does not bounce out.

Since work done on the object is equal to the energy gained by object, energy equal to 'mgh' units is gained by the object. This is the potential energy (PE) of the object. Thus,

PE = mgh

Where,

PE = potential energy is measured in joules (J)

m = mass of the object is measured in kg

g = gravitational acceleration which is equal to 9.8 ms^{-2}

h = perpendicular height from the reference point in m

Gravitational potential energy is the energy of an object due to its position above the surface of the Earth. We often use potential energy where gravitational potential energy is meant.

Example

Find the energy possessed by an object of mass 10 kg when it is at a height of 6 m above the ground. Given, g = 9.8 m s^{-2}.

Solution

Mass of the object,

m = 10 kg

Displacement (height),

h = 6 m Acceleration due to gravity,

g = 9.8 m s^{-2}.

We know,

Potential energy = mgh

= 10 kg × 9.8 m s^{-2} × 6 m

= 588 J.

Degree Celsius and degree Fahrenheit are different but minus 40 degrees Celsius is exactly the same temperature as minus 40 degrees Fahrenheit.

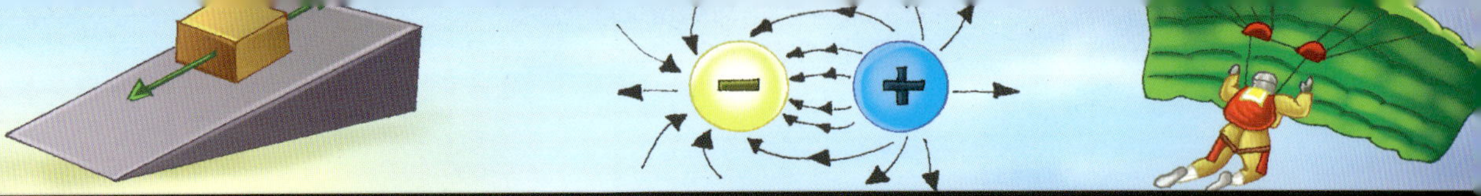

Kinetic energy

The kinetic energy of an object is the energy created due to its motion. The faster an object moves, the more kinetic energy it has. Thus, kinetic energy is dependent on the velocity of the object. Similarly, it also depends on the mass of the object. We generally represent it by KE. Mathematically, the kinetic energy of a point mass m is given by

$KE = \frac{1}{2} mv^2$

It is very clear from the above equation that the kinetic energy of an object is directly proportional to the square of its speed. It means that for a two fold increase in speed, the kinetic energy will increase by a factor of four (square of two). Similarly, for a threefold increase in speed, the kinetic energy will increase by a factor of nine and so on. The kinetic energy of an object is also directly proportional to its mass. Thus, more is mass of a moving object; more is its kinetic energy.

Shot put competition

Fill water balloons with water until they are about the size of tennis balls. These will be used as 'shot'. Holding the shot near your neck, throw it into the air by extending your arm. Measure how far it lands, using the puddle of water from the impact as a marker. The furthest throw wins.

Kinetic energy is a scalar quantity; it does not have a direction. Unlike velocity, acceleration, force and momentum, the kinetic energy of an object is completely described by magnitude alone. Like work and potential energy, the standard unit of kinetic energy is also Joule.

It is now clear that kinetic energy is an expression of the fact that a moving object can do work on anything it hits. The kinetic energy is quantified as the amount of work the object could do as a result of its motion. The total energy of an object is the sum of its kinetic energy and potential energy.

Example

An object of mass 150 kg is moving with a uniform velocity of 10 m s^{-1}. What is the kinetic energy possessed by the object?

Solution

Mass of the object,

$m = 150$ kg,

Velocity of the object,

$v = 10 \text{ m s}^{-1}$

We know that,

$$KE = \frac{1}{2} mv^2$$
$$= \frac{1}{2} * 150 * (10*10)$$
$$= 75*100$$
$$= 7500 \text{ J}$$

Thus, the kinetic energy of the object is 7500 J.

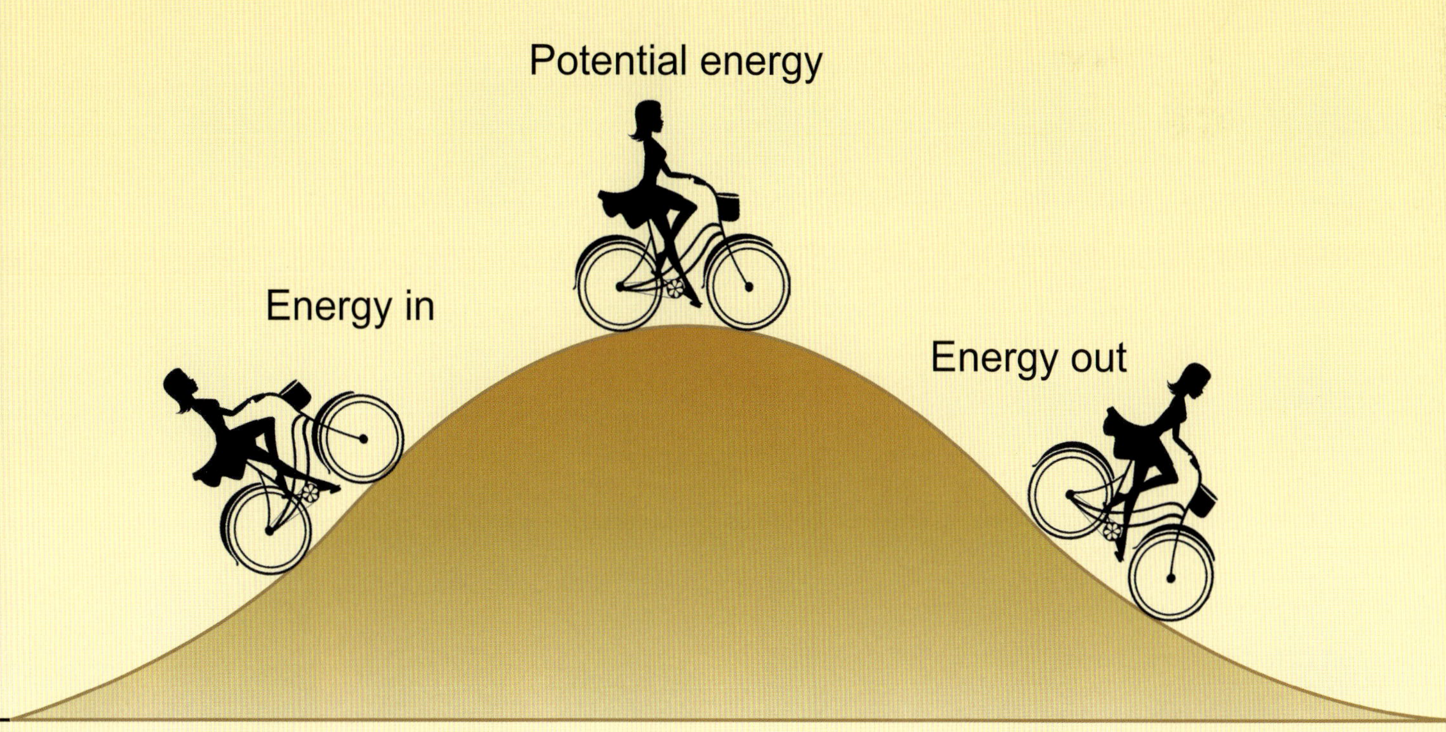

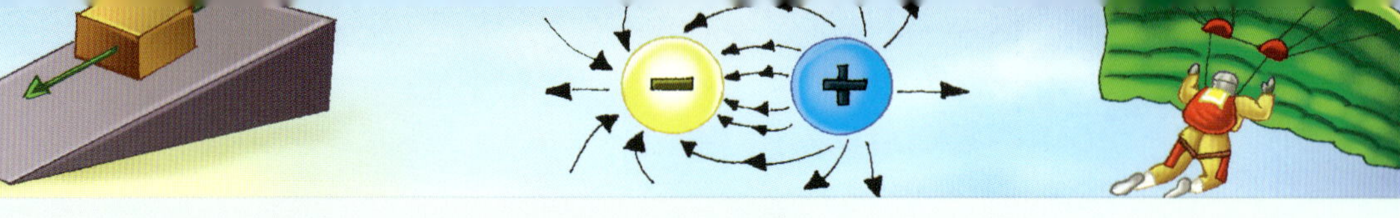

Mechanical energy

Mechanical energy is defined as the sum of potential and kinetic energy associated with any system. Mechanical energy is represented by symbol 'U'. Mathematically, it can be expressed as

$$U = PE + KE$$

From previous equations, we know that

$$PE = mgh$$

$$KE = 1/2\ mv^2$$

Thus,

$$U = mgh + \tfrac{1}{2}\ mv^2$$

Conservation of mechanical energy

The law of conservation of energy states that energy can neither be created nor be destroyed, but is merely converted from one form into another. In a closed system, where there are no external forces acting, the mechanical energy always remains constant. In other words, it does not change. This is called the law of conservation of mechanical energy. This law states that,

"Mechanical energy of a system is constant if the system has only gravitational forces or in an otherwise idealized system which lacks dissipative forces, such as friction and air resistance."

If we consider an example of a swinging pendulum, it has its greatest kinetic energy and least potential energy in the vertical position, in which its speed is greatest and its height above the Earth is least. And it has least kinetic energy and greatest potential energy at the extremities of its swing, in which its speed is zero and its height is greatest. During the swinging of pendulum, energy is continuously passing back and forth between the two forms, kinetic energy and potential energy. If we neglect the friction at the pivot and air resistance, the sum of the kinetic and potential energies of the pendulum, or its mechanical energy, at every instant is constant.

Whenever energy gets transformed, the total energy of the system always remains unchanged. The law of conservation of energy

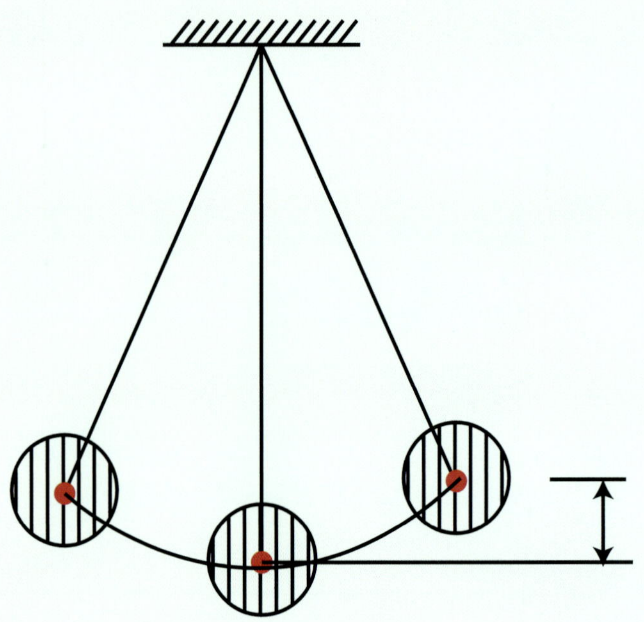

is valid in all situations and for all kinds of transformations.

Let us consider a simple example of a free falling object. Suppose an object of mass 'm' falls freely from a height 'h'. We know that in the beginning, the potential energy is 'mgh' and kinetic energy is zero. The kinetic energy is zero because its velocity is zero. Thus, the total energy or mechanical energy of the object is also 'mgh'. As it falls, its potential energy will change into kinetic energy. If v is the velocity of the object at a given instant, the kinetic energy will be $\frac{1}{2}mv^2$. As the fall of the object continues, the potential energy will decrease and the kinetic energy will increase. When the object is about to reach the ground, h = 0, velocity of object will be maximum. Therefore, the kinetic energy would be the largest and potential energy will be the least.

However, the sum of the potential energy and kinetic energy of the object at all points will be the same. That is,

Potential energy + kinetic energy = constant

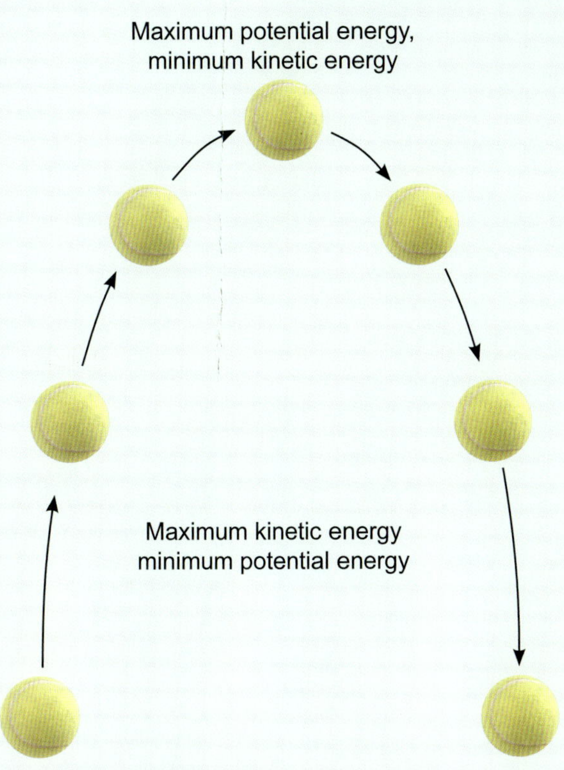

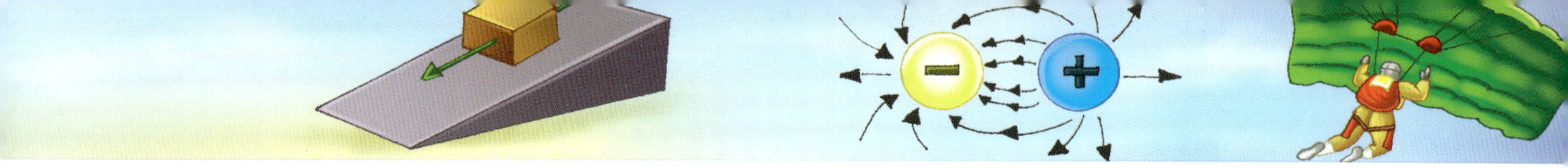

Power

Work has nothing to do with the amount of time that this force acts to cause the displacement. Sometimes, the work is done very quickly and other times the work is done rather slowly. The two people might do the same amount of work, but in considerably different times. The quantity that has to do with the rate at which a certain amount of work is done is known as the power.

Thus, Power is defined as the rate at which work is done. It is the work/time ratio. Mathematically, it is expressed as,

Power = work/ time

P = W/t

The standard metric unit of power is Watt. By implying the above equation for power, we can say that a unit of power is equivalent to a unit of work divided by a unit of time. Thus, 1 Watt is equivalent to 1 Joule/second. It means that 1 watt is the power of an agent, which does work at the rate of 1 joule per second. In other words, we can also say that power is 1 W when the rate of consumption of energy is 1 J s^{-1}.

1 watt = 1 joule/second or 1 W = 1 J s^{-1}.

We express larger rates of energy transfer in kilowatts (kW).

1 kilowatt = 1000 watts

1 kW = 1000 J s–1

For historical reasons, the horsepower is generally used to describe the power delivered by a machine. One horsepower is

equivalent to approximately 750 Watts.

Let us elaborate the equation of power,

Power = work/ time

We know that, work =force * displacement

Thus, Power= force* displacement/ time

Again, we know that,

velocity = displacement / time

We have, power = force * velocity

From this equation of power, we can easily understand that a powerful machine is both strong (because it will be having more force) and fast (due to high velocity). Thus, the power of a machine is directly proportional to its force and velocity. A machine's power is defined by the fact how strong it is to apply a big force to cause a displacement in a small amount of time. If we look into the real life, a powerful weightlifter is strong and fast. Also, a player is always considered powerful in a football team if he is strong and fast.

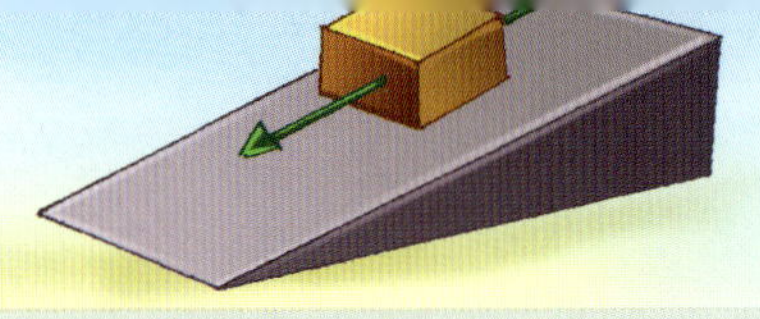
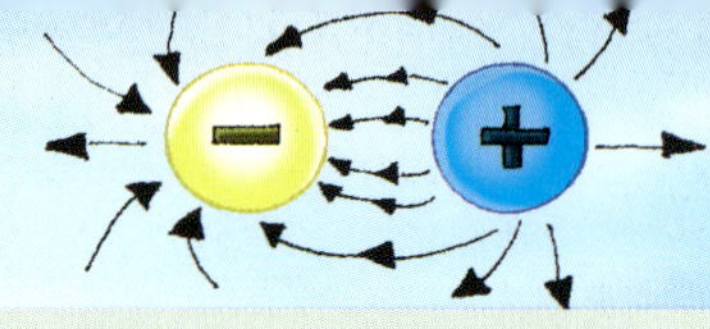

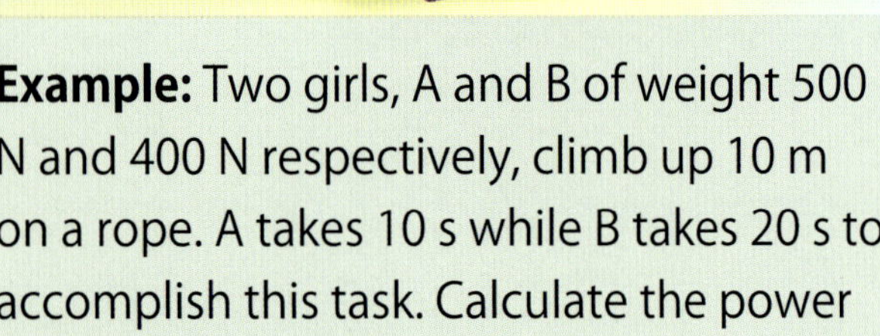

Example: Two girls, A and B of weight 500 N and 400 N respectively, climb up 10 m on a rope. A takes 10 s while B takes 20 s to accomplish this task. Calculate the power expended by each girl.

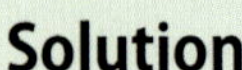

Solution

Power expended by girl A:

Weight of the girl,

$mg = 500$ N

Displacement or the height,

$h = 10$ m

Time taken,

$t = 20$ s

We know that,

Power,

P = Work done/time taken

$= mgh/t$

$= 500$ N $\times$ 10 m/10s

$= 500$ W

Similarly, Power expended by girl B:

Weight of the girl,

$mg = 400$ N

Displacement or the height, $h = 10$ m

Time taken,

$t = 20$ s

We know that,

Power,

P = Work done/time taken

$= mgh/t$

$= 400$ N $\times$ 10 m/20s

$= 200$ W

Power expended by girl A and B is 500 W and 200 W respectively.

Test Your MEMORY

1. Define force. How do we calculate force applied on an object?
2. Define various types of forces.
3. What is the universal law of gravitational force?
4. What is the difference between potential energy and kinetic energy?
5. What do you understand by mechanical energy of an object?
6. What is the difference between mass and weight of a body?
7. How do we define work? Give its mathematical expression.
8. What is the unit of power?
9. What is friction?
10. What is energy? List some of the common sources of energy.
11. What does the second law of motion state about force?
12. What is the unit of force?

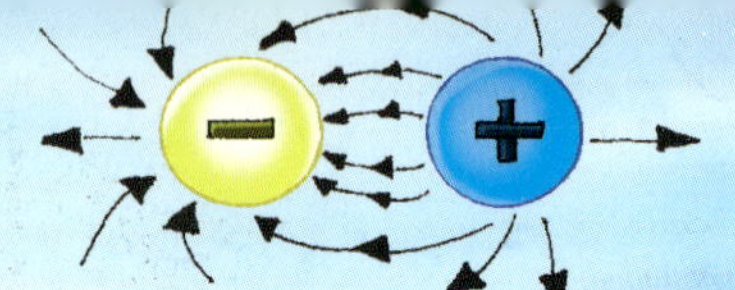

Index